Tides of the Heart

Copyright © 2024 Creative Arts Management OÜ
All rights reserved.

Author: Vivian Laurent
ISBN HARDBACK: 978-9916-90-000-0
ISBN PAPERBACK: 978-9916-90-001-7

The Pull of Celestial Bodies

In the night sky, stars align,
Drawing the eyes, a cosmic sign.
Planets dance in a silent waltz,
Gravity whispers, it never halts.

The moon glows bright, a silver guise,
Tides respond to her gentle cries.
Each orbit a promise, a gravitational thread,
Connecting the heavens where dreams are fed.

Comets streak with fiery tails,
Carrying stories through cosmic trails.
The galaxies spin in a dark embrace,
A ballet of light in the vastest space.

We are stardust, bound by the same force,
Orbiting hopes on a universal course.
In the pull of wonders, we find our place,
A celestial dance in the infinite space.

Singed Sand and Heartstrings

The sun descends with fiery grace,
Burned footprints linger, leaving trace.
A whisper from the ocean wide,
Where dreams and fates collide.

A Sea of Yearning

Waves roll in, with secrets deep,
Each one carries hearts to keep.
The horizon calls, a distant sigh,
Underneath the endless sky.

The Clash of Waves and Wishes

Wishes cast upon the shore,
Lost in tides forevermore.
With every crash, a story spins,
Where hope begins, and sorrow thins.

Ripples in the Silence

In stillness lies a gentle sound,
Whispers rise from underground.
Each ripple breaks the quiet night,
A dance of shadows, soft and light.

Rising and Falling Passions

Hearts ignite in a fleeting glow,
Words exchanged, sweet and low.
Waves of love, the highs and lows,
In a dance where time only slows.

Burning bright, then fading fast,
Moments cherished, none to last.
Yet in the ebb, a lesson learned,
Through the smolder, affection burned.

Driftwood Memories

Nature's whispers in the breeze,
Echoes linger beneath the trees.
Driftwood paths that memories trace,
Time carved lines on a weathered face.

Waves carry whispers from afar,
Every piece tells a hidden scar.
In the silent gold of dusk's embrace,
We find solace in nature's grace.

The Undercurrent of Us

Beneath the surface, currents swirl,
In hidden depths, our dreams unfurl.
Soft glances pass like silent streams,
Entwined in the fabric of shared dreams.

Tides may twist, and shadows play,
Yet, our hearts know the way.
Through tangled roots and whispered trust,
We navigate the depths, as we must.

Moonlit Reflections

Silvery beams on a quiet lake,
Candles flicker, and shadows quake.
Whispers soft in the midnight air,
Beneath the stars, dreams laid bare.

Ripples dance under the moon's gaze,
Catching memories in a gentle haze.
In the stillness, our thoughts collide,
Finding peace where our hearts reside.

Beyond the Tempest

Winds howled fiercely, skies turned grey,
Hearts felt heavy, lost in the fray.
Yet within the chaos, a whisper came,
Hope ignited, still burning flame.

Through the storm's rage, we dared to dream,
Against the current, we formed a team.
Bound by a vision, unwavering and bright,
We sailed beyond, into the light.

Ensconced in the Lagoon

Nestled in stillness, the waters gleam,
Reflecting the whispers of a gentle dream.
Palms sway softly, a serene embrace,
Time slows down in this tranquil space.

Ripples dance lightly, kissed by the breeze,
Nature's own canvas, aimed to please.
In this haven, all worries cease,
A moment of solace, a moment of peace.

A Driftwood Reflection

Washed ashore, the wood lies bare,
A story untold, in the salty air.
Each knot and curve, a journey's trace,
Tales of the ocean, held in embrace.

Life flows onward, just like the tide,
With every ebb, we learn and abide.
Treasures of time, in grains of sand,
Lessons keep drifting, like the wood on land.

Roots of Emotion in the Sand

Beneath the surface, deep and wide,
Emotions entwined where secrets hide.
Roots stretch downward, searching for light,
Yearning for connection, in the night.

Footprints washed away, yet souls remain,
In the dance of the waves, joy and pain.
Together they flourish, a silent command,
Life's bittersweet song, in the shifting sand.

Submerged Sentiments

Beneath the waves, feelings reside,
Lost in the depths, where dreams collide.
Silent whispers, secrets concealed,
In the ocean's arms, truths revealed.

An anchor weighs on the heart's tide,
Hope floats softly, a gentle guide.
Drowned in shades of blue and gray,
Submerged sentiments drift away.

Sailors of the Soul

With every dawn, they set their quest,
Navigating storms, seeking rest.
Stars above, a guiding light,
Sailors of the soul, through the night.

Their hearts the compass, wildly free,
Charting the course of destiny.
Each wave a story, lost and found,
In the vast ocean, their dreams abound.

Cascading Emotions

Like waterfalls, feelings rush down,
Tears and laughter in layers drown.
Moments fleeting, like a stream,
Cascading emotions, a vivid dream.

Ripples form where hearts collide,
With every drop, feelings abide.
Flowing freely, wild and true,
In the currents, I find you.

Shores of Solitude

Upon the sands, I walk alone,
Waves whisper secrets of the unknown.
The horizon stretches, vast and wide,
On the shores of solitude, I confide.

Each grain of sand, a memory cast,
Time moves slowly, yet seems so fast.
In quiet moments, thoughts take flight,
On the shores of solitude, I find light.

Sailing Through Memories

The whispers of the ocean breeze,
Carry tales from yesteryears.
With every wave, a distant sigh,
And twinkling stars above me lie.

In boats of dreams, we drift along,
Past islands where our hearts belong.
The salty air, a sweet embrace,
In every rush, I find my place.

The horizon calls with colors bright,
Reminding me of love's first light.
Each cresting tide brings back the past,
A fleeting moment, forever cast.

I sail on seas of joy and pain,
Through storms of doubt, in sunshine's reign.
As memories unfold like sails,
I chart my course where love prevails.

The Hidden Reefs of Love

Beneath the waves, the beauty lies,
In coral beds where silence cries.
The hidden reefs await our touch,
An underwater world, so much.

We navigate through life's embrace,
In depths where time can leave no trace.
With every glance, a spark ignites,
In shadows deep, love's heart delights.

Unseen currents pull us near,
Yet through the chaos, there's no fear.
For in the depths, we find our way,
As heartbeats blend with ocean's sway.

Together we explore the deep,
Where secrets of the sea still sleep.
In hidden reefs, our hearts will soar,
Forever drawn to love's great shore.

Soundtrack of the Sea

A symphony of waves at play,
The ocean sings both night and day.
With every splash and gentle swell,
The music of the sea, we dwell.

In rhythms bold, the tides recede,
A violin of breeze, a steady heed.
Each crested wave, a song of old,
In every note, a tale retold.

The seagulls cry, a fleeting tune,
Beneath the watchful sun and moon.
The heartbeat of the shore entwined,
A melody that frees the mind.

As I drift on, the notes surround,
In ocean's arms, my heart is found.
For in this concert, wild and free,
I lose myself, the soul of sea.

Caught in the Undertow

In currents strong, I lose my way,
The undertow has come to play.
With every pull, I fight and strain,
Yet love's deep water holds the chain.

I tumble down, then rise to breathe,
With every wave, there's more to cleave.
The depths below, a siren's call,
In darkened seas, I risk it all.

The ebb and flow of heart's desire,
In salty depths, my hopes transpire.
Though fear may drown my truest song,
I find the strength to carry on.

Through undertows, I seek the light,
In shadows deep, I'll stand and fight.
For love will guide me through the storm,
In ocean's heart, I'll find my form.

Letters in a Bottle

Waves whisper secrets down the shore,
Ink and paper drift, tales to explore.
In bottles cast, dreams take flight,
Hopes and wishes, lost in the night.

With every tide, they're drawn to land,
Messages hidden in grains of sand.
Hearts once broken, now mended true,
Each letter a spark for me and you.

The ocean's breath carries them far,
Stories entwined beneath the stars.
Fate and fortune, old as the sea,
In these bottles, we'll both be free.

The Shoreline of Belonging

Where the sea kisses the golden shore,
A sense of peace, forever more.
The tides embrace, a gentle roam,
Here in the waves, I find my home.

Footprints linger, washed away,
Memories etched in the light of day.
Seagulls cry as they dance above,
This sacred space, a place of love.

Shells whisper stories of days gone by,
Under the vast and endless sky.
In the sand, I write my song,
A melody sweet where I belong.

Sandcastles and Heartbeats

In the warm sun, we build our dreams,
Sandcastles rise, or so it seems.
With every scoop and careful hand,
A kingdom grows upon the sand.

As the tide creeps closer to our feet,
Heartbeats quicken, swift and sweet.
Laughter mingles with the ocean's roar,
In this moment, I couldn't ask for more.

Each wave that crashes, a fleeting chance,
To dance with time, a summer romance.
Yet with each tide, our castles fall,
But in our hearts, we'll have it all.

The Swells of Tomorrow

With whispers of dreams on the salty breeze,
The ocean yields its promises with ease.
Each swell that breaks speaks of our fate,
In the waters deep, we contemplate.

Tomorrow's waves bring hope anew,
In shades of azure and vibrant blue.
Riding the currents of what's to come,
A journey awaits, to which we're numb.

As the sun sets on the horizon wide,
We find our strength in the ebb and tide.
Together we'll brave the storms ahead,
The swells of tomorrow, where dreams are fed.

Lighthouse Lament

A beacon stands tall, the night wears thin,
Guarding the shores where memories begin.
Waves crash below with thunderous might,
While shadows dance dimly in the fading light.

Forgotten whispers echo in the gale,
Stories of ships that dared to set sail.
The lighthouse keeper, weary and wise,
Watches the tide with a sorrowful sigh.

Crashing Waves

Salt and foam crash upon the stone,
Nature's fierce song, a mighty droning tone.
Each wave a story, a tale of the sea,
A rhythm of life, wild and free.

The tempest roars, the ocean fights back,
Seagulls cry out, riding the black.
In each swell and dip, we find our place,
In the heart of the storm, a tranquil embrace.

Whispered Dreams

In twilight's glow, hopes softly bloom,
Secret desires in the still of the room.
Gentle breezes carry the sighs,
Of whispered dreams and starlit skies.

Silent wishes float like leaves,
Dancing on air, where the night weaves.
Fleeting moments hold weight so dear,
In the quiet, we conquer our fear.

The Depths of Tenderness

In the heart's abyss, where kindness flows,
Tenderness lingers like a gentle rose.
Every touch a promise, every glance a song,
In the warmth of love, we know we belong.

Deep as the ocean, vast as the sky,
In moments shared, we learn to fly.
The depths we explore, hand in hand we dive,
In the embrace of truth, we feel alive.

Navigating the Unknown

Charting the seas where shadows loom,
We sail through horizons, embracing the gloom.
Stars are our guide, the compass our friend,
Through storms we venture, with hearts that won't bend.

Each wave a challenge, each gust a quest,
In the face of fear, we stand up and best.
For in the unknown, we find our way,
A journey of courage, come what may.

Salty Kisses at Dusk

Waves whisper softly to the shore,
As the sun dips low, opening the door.
Eyes meet in the twilight's embrace,
Salty kisses, time cannot erase.

The breeze carries secrets from afar,
Filling the night with dreams ajar.
Footprints in sand, our story unfolds,
As dusk wraps us in threads of gold.

Stars begin to twinkle above,
A symphony of the sea, a song of love.
Each moment cherished, a treasure to hold,
Our hearts dance gently, brave and bold.

Together we stand, under velvet skies,
Bathed in the twilight, where magic lies.
With salty kisses, forever we'll trust,
In this fleeting moment, in love we must.

The Pull of Your Presence

Your laughter is a gentle tide,
Pulling me closer, I cannot hide.
In every heartbeat, I feel the sway,
The pull of your presence, night and day.

Eyes like the ocean, deep and true,
In their depths, I find my view.
A compass that guides me through the night,
With you by my side, the world feels right.

Words unspoken, yet so clear,
Each glance shared, drawing us near.
The warmth of your touch lights a spark,
In the silence, you chase away the dark.

Together we drift on this endless sea,
The pull of your presence is home to me.
With the stars as our map, let's wander free,
In this beautiful dance, just you and me.

Oceans of Longing

Between us lies oceans of longing,
A vast expanse, our hearts are thronging.
Each wave a wish, crashing on the shore,
Echoes of dreams that we can't ignore.

The tides rise high, pulling at my soul,
In the distance, I can feel you whole.
An endless journey through the moonlight glow,
In the depths of the ocean, love will flow.

With every sunset, I feel your call,
A siren's song through the rise and fall.
The currents swirl with whispered grace,
In the sea of my heart, you've found your place.

Though miles apart, I know you're near,
Oceans of longing, yet I hold you dear.
With every tide, I'll sail and soar,
In love's embrace, forevermore.

Distant Horizons of Hope

At the edge of the sea, horizons await,
Distant and shimmering, a beckoning fate.
With every sunrise, new dreams ignite,
Whispers of hope in the morning light.

Clouds may gather, shadows may fall,
Yet through the storm, love answers the call.
Together we'll wander, hearts intertwined,
Distant horizons, our souls aligned.

Each step we take is a step towards grace,
In the arms of the sea, we find our place.
No matter how far, together we'll cope,
Flying on wings of our infinite hope.

The compass of stars leads us on,
Through twilight's hues, till the night is gone.
With dreams in our hearts, we'll never stop,
To reach those horizons, we rise to the top.

Beneath the Surface of You

In quiet depths where shadows play,
I find reflections of the day.
Your laughter sings in muted tones,
Echoes whisper among the stones.

The world above may seem so bright,
But here, it's calm, a gentle light.
I trace the lines that time has drawn,
In currents where my heart is drawn.

Beneath the surface, dreams entwine,
A secret realm that's yours and mine.
The waves may rise, the tides may shift,
Yet in this space, our souls uplift.

So let me dive, let me explore,
The hidden parts I long to adore.
For in these depths, I truly see,
The beauty that you are to me.

Waters of Time and Memory

Ripples form on tranquil streams,
Carrying whispers of our dreams.
Memories flow like gentle tides,
In the heart where love abides.

Each wave that breaks upon the shore,
Holds fragments of the days before.
In every droplet, stories gleam,
Woven softly in a dream.

The past may fade like distant stars,
Yet, here we stand, beneath the scars.
We navigate this timeless sea,
Finding solace, you and me.

Through currents swift and waters deep,
In silent vows, our secrets keep.
The streams of time will never cease,
In every wave, we find our peace.

Windswept Words

Whispers carried on the breeze,
Tell of moments, hearts at ease.
Every sigh, a soft embrace,
Lost in time's unfathomed space.

The world spins round, a dance of light,
Yet here I stand, in quiet flight.
Thoughts like feathers drift away,
Through open skies, they softly sway.

With every wind that bends the trees,
I find the truth in mysteries.
Words unspoken roam the air,
Searching for a heart that dares.

In the gusts, we weave our dreams,
Chasing shadows, silver beams.
So let us shout, let voices soar,
For in the wind, we ask for more.

Shoreline Secrets

Footprints left in soft, warm sand,
Trace the path of where we stand.
Whispers carried by the tide,
Hold the secrets we confide.

The ocean breathes, a timeless song,
In its embrace, we both belong.
Salt and spray, the fragrance sweet,
A melody that feels complete.

With every wave, the world drifts by,
Yet here we dream beneath the sky.
In twilight hues, our laughter rings,
As evening calls on whispering wings.

The shoreline holds our stories near,
Capturing moments, ever dear.
In every crest, our hopes arise,
Finding magic in sunset skies.

Moonlit Murmurs

Whispers from the silver night,
Gentle echoes, soft and bright.
Stars above in silent dance,
Hearts entwined, we take our chance.

Shadows twist in playful grace,
In the dark, we've found our place.
Every sigh a secret shared,
In moonlit beams, love is declared.

Tiny lights burn in the sky,
Underneath, two souls will fly.
Ocean waves sing lullabies,
In this calm, our passion lies.

Crickets serenade the night,
As cradled dreams take gentle flight.
In your gaze, the world falls still,
In moonlit murmurs, hearts will thrill.

Uncharted Waters of Affection

Sailing through an endless sea,
Each wave holds a mystery.
Hearts navigated by the moon,
In these depths, love's gentle tune.

Storms may rise, yet sails are set,
No regrets, no room for fret.
With every tide, our hopes will grow,
In uncharted waters, we will flow.

Charting courses, hand in hand,
Together, we will understand.
Every ripple tells our tale,
In affection's breeze, we'll never fail.

Embracing the unknown with cheer,
In our hearts, we hold what's dear.
Boundless journeys, skies so wide,
In these waters, love our guide.

Sailing on Currents of the Past

Memories glide like autumn leaves,
Whispers of time that never grieves.
Wavy lines in faded maps,
Navigating through history's traps.

Echoes linger in the air,
Stories told without a care.
Sailing forth on waves of yore,
In the past, we find our core.

Tides of love that shaped our sails,
Carried forward by heartfelt trails.
Each moment cherished, never lost,
In our journey, we count the cost.

Holding tight to what we've known,
In the currents, seeds are sown.
Bound by threads that time can't sever,
Sailing on, our hearts endeavor.

The Color of Dusk

Blushing skies in shades of rose,
As the day gently dozes.
Hues of amber kiss the night,
In this moment, pure delight.

Whispers soft as twilight creeps,
In this hour, the world sleeps.
Colors blend, a soft embrace,
In dusk's warmth, we find our space.

Every shadow tells a tale,
In twilight's glow, we will prevail.
Fading light, a painter's hand,
As we dream, together we stand.

Wrapped in dusk's tender sighs,
Promises blend with midnight skies.
In these colors, love is found,
In the dusk, our hearts are bound.

Shifting Sands of Love

In the warmth of twilight's glow,
Two souls dance, ebb and flow.
Whispers soft like desert winds,
Time unravels, love begins.

Footprints fade in golden grains,
Hearts entwined through joys and pains.
With every kiss, a promise made,
In the dunes where dreams cascade.

But storms will come to test the bond,
Yet through the shadows, we'll respond.
In shifting sands, we stand as one,
Our love a blaze, a constant sun.

Through ebbs of time, our spirits soar,
Across the ages, forevermore.
In every grain, a memory holds,
Shifting sands, a tale retold.

Echoes in the Depths

In the stillness where waters meet,
Deep down lies a heartbeat sweet.
Whispers carried on the tide,
Lost loves linger, never hide.

Fathoms deep, where shadows play,
Secrets of night, kept at bay.
In caverns dark, the echoes sing,
Of hearts that felt the pulse of spring.

Ripples stretch across the night,
Each one a memory in flight.
With every surge, a tale unfolds,
Of fleeting warmth and love so bold.

Yet from the depths, a light will gleam,
Guiding souls through every dream.
In the silence, we hear the call,
Echoes of love, embracing all.

The Pull of Yearning

In distant lands where shadows dwell,
A heart is caught in longing's spell.
The stars above, a map to trace,
Each twinkle pulls, a sweet embrace.

Between the whispers of the night,
A longing stirs, a flame ignites.
With every sigh, the moonlight beams,
Guiding us through woven dreams.

The tides of fate, they ebb and flow,
A magnetic force we both know.
In every glance, in every touch,
Yearning deepens, it means so much.

Yet in the distance, fear may play,
Will love endure, or drift away?
But in our hearts, a promise stays,
To follow love through endless days.

A Sea of Dreams

Beneath the waves, where silence thrives,
A sea of dreams, where hope derives.
Each wave a wish, each tide a song,
In this vast place, we all belong.

Sailing forth on currents bright,
Chasing stars that paint the night.
In gentle lulls, our spirits rest,
The ocean's heart beats in our chest.

Together we will navigate,
A journey forged by love and fate.
In every storm, we find our way,
Through trials faced, come what may.

On shores of hope, we'll plant the seed,
A love that grows, a timeless creed.
In this sea, our dreams will gleam,
Forever anchored in the dream.

The Call of Distant Horizons

Beyond the hills where shadows play,
A whisper floats with skies of gray.
The sun dips low, the stars ignite,
Inviting dreams to take their flight.

Each step we take, a path unfolds,
With heartbeats strong and tales untold.
The winds of change, they beckon now,
To distant shores, we make our vow.

A shimmering sea, the open wide,
An endless journey, a longing tide.
With every wave, we chart the way,
To find our truth, come what may.

In every sunset, a promise holds,
Of places new and stories bold.
We're drawn to where the wild hearts roam,
The call of horizons, leading us home.

Waves of Emotion

In gentle tides, our feelings surge,
A dance of thoughts, a silent urge.
With every ebb, a secret sigh,
Each wave that breaks whispers goodbye.

The ocean deep holds treasures rare,
Moments lost in the salted air.
When joy cascades, or sadness reigns,
We ride the swell of love's terrains.

From calm reflections to storms within,
The heart's vast sea where dreams begin.
We surf the highs, we brave the lows,
In this vast world, our passion grows.

Each wave that crashes on the shore,
Brings forth the pulse we can't ignore.
In every tide, we learn to trust,
Waves of emotion, a bond so just.

Currents of Desire

Beneath the surface, whispers grow,
A current strong, a secret flow.
With longing glances, we entwine,
In hidden depths, our souls align.

Through tangled dreams, we drift and glide,
With every heartbeat, hope and pride.
As shadows flicker, lights ignite,
In currents of desire, we take flight.

Each brush of hands, a spark, a flame,
Unveiling truths we dare not name.
In the silent space, our spirits blend,
With every touch, we dare transcend.

The flow of night, the dawn's embrace,
In pulsing rhythm, we find our place.
Riding the tide, we chase the stars,
Currents of desire, our guiding cars.

The Rhythm of Affection

In every beat, a tender call,
A melody that binds us all.
Through highs and lows, we find our way,
The rhythm of affection holds sway.

Your laughter rings, a sweet refrain,
Echoing softly through joy and pain.
With every glance, a song is spun,
Together we dance, two hearts as one.

In whispers shared, our secrets bloom,
In cozy corners, love finds room.
With every heartbeat, the ties grow strong,
In this embrace, we both belong.

The rhythm flows, like water pure,
With every moment, our love endures.
In harmony, we face the night,
The rhythm of affection, our guiding light.

Flowing Affections

In the garden blooms so bright,
Hearts entwined in soft twilight.
Gentle whispers, love's sweet call,
Like a river, we conquer all.

Hands a-glow, with warm embrace,
Moments cherished, time can't erase.
In every heartbeat, passion grows,
Like the petals, love bestows.

Dreams are woven in the night,
Stars above, our guiding light.
Together, we will find our way,
Through flowing affections, come what may.

Whispers of the Abyss

In shadows deep, the secrets dwell,
Whispers echo, casting a spell.
A haunting dance within the dark,
Flickers dim, but still ignite the spark.

The ocean's breath, a secret shore,
Where time stands still, forevermore.
Voices call from depths unknown,
In the abyss, the heart has grown.

Through twilight mist, I hear their sighs,
Guiding me beneath the skies.
In every tide, a tale unfolds,
Of whispers lost, and love it holds.

The Dance of Desires

In the moonlight, shadows sway,
Yearning hearts that seek to play.
With every touch, electric fire,
We lose ourselves in dance of desire.

A heartbeat quickens, breaths align,
In this moment, you are mine.
With every glance, the world slows down,
As we twirl beneath the crown.

Through the night, our spirits fly,
In the rhythm, you and I.
Entwined, we leap against the stars,
In this dance, our souls are ours.

Stars Beneath the Waves

Dancing light on ocean's crest,
Whispers of the deep, a quest.
Stars reflecting in silver swells,
Secrets hidden, the water tells.

With every wave, a story flows,
A reminder of where love grows.
In the depths, our dreams reside,
With stars beneath, the currents glide.

As tides embrace the sandy shore,
We find the magic, evermore.
In the twilight, worlds collide,
Stars beneath the waves, our guide.

Navigating Unknown Waters

In the mist where shadows play,
We sail forth, come what may.
Stars above are our guide,
In the waves, we confide.

With a compass that's worn down,
We brave storms, no frown.
The currents pull and sway,
Yet hope lights our way.

Each wave a lesson learned,
With each tide, a heart yearned.
In the unknown, we find grace,
In every challenging place.

Together we chart our course,
In the depths, find our source.
As horizons stretch and bend,
We sail on 'til the end.

Ripples of Connection

A pebble dropped, a circle forms,
Ripples dance in all storms.
In the stillness, bonds grow,
A quiet strength, soft glow.

With each touch, a silent pact,
Finding beauty in the act.
In the shimmer, hearts align,
A connection, pure and fine.

Voices blend like gentle streams,
Intertwined like whispered dreams.
In the distance, laughter rings,
Together the joy it brings.

Through the waters, wide and free,
Unity in you and me.
In every wave, a shared breath,
Love transcends, conquers death.

Fragments of the Ocean

Glimmers of light on deep blue,
Shards of stories, old and new.
Each wave a memory cast,
Fragments of a distant past.

Seashells whisper tales of lore,
Echoes from the ocean's floor.
In every grain of sand's embrace,
Lie the dreams of time and space.

Rippling surface, secrets kept,
Where the ancient waters wept.
From the depths, we glean the throng,
In the fragments, we belong.

As we wander shore to shore,
Gathering treasures, evermore.
Each fragment, a piece of home,
In the sea, we are not alone.

High and Low Affairs

Up above, where eagles soar,
Dreams take flight, we long for more.
Gravity holds our feet to ground,
In the heights, our souls are found.

Low beneath, where currents swirl,
Life teems bright, mysteries unfurl.
In the depths, shadows glide,
Yet beauty blooms as dreams collide.

Through valleys deep and mountains grand,
We navigate with steady hand.
In each affair, a tale unfolds,
In whispers soft, life beholds.

High and low, a balance sought,
In every struggle, knowledge taught.
As we rise, we also fall,
In this dance, we find our call.

Remnants of a Rising Tide

Whispers of water kiss the shore,
Memories linger, forevermore.
Footprints washed away by time,
Echoes of laughter, soft as a rhyme.

Seashells scattered, secrets untold,
Stories in grains of sand unfold.
Each wave a chapter, a tale to share,
Remnants of love linger in the air.

The sun dips low, a fiery glow,
Casting shadows where dreams float slow.
With twilight's grace, the tide retreats,
Leaving behind its bittersweet treats.

In moonlit nights, reflections gleam,
Carried by whispers of a dream.
Rising tides will come once more,
Yet the remnants linger on the shore.

Heartstrings and Ocean Currents

Tangled in the rhythm of waves,
Feelings ride the ocean, free like graves.
Strings that tether, pull and sway,
Hearts adrift in the salty spray.

Anchored dreams beneath the blue,
Current pulls, yet I long for you.
Each crest a promise, each trough a sigh,
Together we float, beneath the sky.

Seagulls call, a mournful tune,
Echoes resonate beneath the moon.
The tide reveals what love can show,
With every pulse, the heart will grow.

In the depths, a light will shine,
Navigating through each tangled line.
Heartstrings pulling through the depths,
Boundless love, with every breath.

Embracing the Undertow

Subtle forces pull below,
Hidden currents, soft and slow.
Wrapped in shadows, lost in dreams,
Embracing every silent scream.

Tides of change whisper to me,
A dance with fate, wild and free.
Waves that crash, yet I remain,
In the depths, I feel no pain.

Sinking deeper, finding grace,
In the dark, I find my place.
The undertow, a gentle guide,
Leading me where fears subside.

In the silence, strength will grow,
Lessons learned beneath the flow.
With open arms and heart awake,
Embracing all that tides will take.

Waves of Nostalgia

Tides of memory wash ashore,
Echoes of laughter, tales of yore.
Childhood dreams like driftwood lie,
Brought to life beneath the sky.

Each crest reminds me of the past,
Sweet moments fleeting, yet they last.
Sunset glows on distant waves,
Whispers of losses, yet love saves.

Wanderlust ignites the spirit,
Longing for a time we near it.
Fragments of joy and tears collide,
In waves of nostalgia, we abide.

Surfing through time, I find my way,
In memories bright, I long to stay.
With every wave, my heart does glide,
Through waves of nostalgia, love my guide.

Starlit Serenades

Beneath the night, the stars align,
Whispers of dreams in the air,
A symphony soft, a sweet design,
Hearts united without a care.

Each twinkle sings a melody,
A dance of light, a fleeting spark,
In shadows deep, we wander free,
Guided by love, igniting the dark.

The moon hangs high, a watchful eye,
Casting its glow on paths we tread,
With every breath, together we fly,
In starlit peace, our fears are shed.

So let us dream beneath the sky,
In serenades that softly flow,
With every whisper, we'll never die,
Forever bound in this cosmic glow.

The Call of Distant Shores

Waves crashing softly on grains of sand,
A melody pure, a siren's tune,
Whispers of journeys across the land,
Echoing dreams beneath a silver moon.

Seagulls cry high, greeting the dawn,
A call to wander beyond the blue,
With hearts alight, and worries gone,
The distant shores beckon me and you.

Each tide that rolls, a secret shared,
Adventure awaits with every swell,
In the ocean's arms, we're unprepared,
For tales of love and freedom to tell.

Set sail on winds that dance and spin,
With the horizon promising more,
Let the waves pull us deep within,
In the embrace of distant shores.

Underneath the Foam

Beneath the waves where secrets sleep,
In depths where coral gardens thrive,
Silently calling, the ocean's keep,
Whispers of life, where dreams arrive.

The foam cascades like lace on skin,
A gentle touch from the sea's embrace,
In currents warm, we lose and win,
Finding our rhythm, lost in space.

Shells hidden deep, stories untold,
Mirroring love in their fragile form,
Treasures of time, both new and old,
Awakening hearts in the ocean's storm.

So let us dive into sapphire dreams,
Where echoes of laughter dance and play,
Underneath foam, life's vibrant themes
Breathe new life in a fluid ballet.

The Storm before the Silence

Clouds converge in a brooding sky,
A tempest whispers, the winds grow bold,
Nature's fury, a potent cry,
As thunder rolls, the world unfolds.

Lightning strikes with a brilliant glare,
Illuminating shadows that loom,
Tension builds in electric air,
A dance of chaos, the soul's deep gloom.

Through rain-soaked streets, we find our way,
With every drop, a heartbeat's race,
Yet in the storm, we learn to sway,
Embracing darkness, we find our grace.

For after the storm, the silence hums,
A tranquil pause, a breath of peace,
From raucous cries, the stillness comes,
In nature's arms, we find release.

Heartbeats on the Horizon

In twilight's glow, shadows dance,
Silent whispers take their chance.
Fading light on the sea's embrace,
Hope awakens in this place.

A distant call, the stars align,
Echoing dreams, yours and mine.
With every pulse, our spirits soar,
Together, we can ask for more.

In the silence, a heartbeat sings,
Woven tales of forgotten things.
Across the waves, a promise made,
In love's embrace, we shall not fade.

As dawn breaks bright, fears retreat,
In this moment, our hearts meet.
On horizon's edge, we stand tall,
Bound forever, through it all.

Embracing the Waves

The ocean's breath carries a tune,
A lullaby beneath the moon.
With every crest, a chance to feel,
In salty air, our hearts reveal.

Beneath the surf, secrets lie,
Crashing tides that never die.
Hands entwined, we face the storm,
In storms and calms, our souls keep warm.

Together we dance on shifting sand,
With nature's pulse, we take a stand.
Embracing waves both fierce and mild,
In watery depths, we are beguiled.

As twilight kisses the fading shore,
Each wave a promise, forevermore.
In the rhythm of the rolling sea,
We find our peace, just you and me.

The Mist of Remembrance

In morning light, the fog appears,
Whispers of love, echoing years.
Memories linger, soft and bright,
In the mist, our dreams take flight.

Faces fade, but spirits stay,
Guiding us on our chosen way.
Through the haze, we catch a glance,
A dance of ghosts, a timeless dance.

Each heartbeat wrapped in tender grace,
Time stands still in this sacred space.
Through veils of mist, the past embraces,
In the soft glow of familiar faces.

As shadows blend with the rising sun,
We find the warmth that's never done.
In the mist, life's stories weave,
Heartstrings pull, and we believe.

Sheltering Shores of Emotion

In gentle folds, the land holds fast,
A refuge found, the storms have passed.
Our hearts sail on the tranquil tide,
In sheltering shores, we can confide.

With every wave, a tale unfolds,
Secrets shared, both new and old.
On sandy paths, our laughter rings,
In warm embrace, our spirit sings.

Through shifting sands, we chart our course,
Love's steady hand, our guiding force.
As day turns night, the stars ignite,
Together we shine, our souls alight.

On these shores, we build our dreams,
In quiet moments, life redeems.
With every heartbeat, a bond grows strong,
In sheltering love, we both belong.

Castaway Memories

Whispers of the ocean call,
Fragments of a distant shore.
Footprints lost in shifting sand,
Echoes of the days before.

Chasing sunsets, fleeting light,
Stories folded in the tide.
Each wave sings a different song,
Carrying the dreams denied.

Faded photographs in hand,
Memory's embrace so warm.
Are we not but castaways,
Drifting toward another storm?

In the silence, ghosts reside,
Laughter dances on the breeze.
Haunting notes of summer nights,
A symphony of lost ease.

The ebbs of Yesterday

Time flows like a silent stream,
Yesterday slips from our grasp.
Fleeting moments fade away,
In its depths, our memories clasp.

Each tear falls like autumn leaves,
Carried forth on winds of change.
What was bright now dims with time,
Familiar faces feel so strange.

Pictures yellowed with the years,
Words unspoken linger near.
In the quiet, truths unfold,
Echoes that we long to hear.

Yet in this ebb, we find a spark,
New beginnings rise like dawn.
Yesterday, a guiding light,
Informing paths that we move on.

Currents of Belonging

Together we drift in the night,
Tides bring us close, then apart.
In the heart of the tempest,
We find solace, a shared start.

Waves unite in the moon's glow,
Anchoring our souls as one.
Through every storm that shakes us,
A bond deepens, never done.

Stories woven like a net,
Pulling us from distant shores.
With every rise and fall, we know,
Home is found where spirit soars.

Currents strong, yet gentle hands,
Guiding us through unseen strife.
In the sea of endless dreams,
We discover the threads of life.

Constellations in the Waves

Stars reflect upon the sea,
Guiding ships through velvet skies.
Each ripple holds a secret wish,
Whispered softly in the sighs.

Beneath the surface, stories shine,
Constellations intertwined.
With every crash against the rocks,
Fates and journeys are aligned.

The moon, a lantern in the dark,
Casts its glow on dreams at bay.
In the dance of tides and time,
We find hope in the sway.

Underneath the cosmic show,
Waves embrace our wanderlust.
In each swell and breaking crest,
We learn to follow and trust.

Depths Untold

In shadows deep where secrets lie,
Whispers dance and moments sigh.
The echoes of a past so bold,
In waters dark, the depths untold.

Beneath the surface, life concealed,
A thousand truths remain unrevealed.
With silent strength, the heart withstands,
The currents shaped by fate's own hands.

Like sunken treasures lost in time,
Each heartbeat sings a silent rhyme.
For every tear, a lesson spun,
In depths unknown, our journey's run.

Yet through the dark, a spark ignites,
A beacon held in starry nights.
With courage found in dreams retold,
We brave the waves, our depths unfold.

Celestial Currents

Beneath the stars, where dreams take flight,
The cosmos breathes in soft twilight.
Galaxies swirl in cosmic dance,
Guiding souls with a glance.

In every pulse, the universe sings,
Whispers of hope on ethereal wings.
Through voids of time, we drift and sway,
Lost yet found, we chart our way.

The stardust calls, a siren's song,
In celestial realms, we all belong.
Mapping journeys on a vast expanse,
We ride the waves of circumstance.

So let us flow like rivers bright,
With hearts alive in the endless night.
For in the currents, life unfolds,
In celestial dreams, the future holds.

A Heart Adrift

A heart adrift on silent seas,
Winds of change sway with such ease.
Forgotten shores seem far away,
As tides of time begin to play.

The compass spins; the stars align,
In search of love, a voice divine.
Each wave that crashes holds a sigh,
A silent wish that dares to fly.

Beneath the sky, both vast and wide,
We navigate with hope as guide.
Through storms and calm, the journey's long,
Yet in our hearts, we find the song.

For every tear a lesson learned,
In every turn, a flame discerned.
With open hearts, we chart our path,
A heart adrift, embracing wrath.

Beneath the Changing Skies

Beneath the skies of shifting hue,
We chase the dreams that feel so true.
With every dawn, new colors bloom,
While shadows dance in twilight's room.

The clouds will part, the stars will gleam,
Within our hearts, the fires beam.
Together, we explore the vast,
In moments fleeting, hold them fast.

With laughter bright and smiles wide,
We navigate the rising tide.
As seasons change and time will flow,
In every heart, the stories grow.

So let us bask beneath these skies,
With open hearts and hopeful eyes.
For in this world, both wild and free,
We find our place, just you and me.

Whispers on the Shore

Softly the waves call out to me,
The sea breeze carries a melody.
Footprints in sand tell tales untold,
As whispers of secrets begin to unfold.

Shells gather memories, bright and clear,
Every tide lingers, drawing me near.
Sunset paints skies with hues of gold,
In the hush of the evening, dreams take hold.

The moonlight dances on the crest of waves,
Guarding the love that the ocean saves.
Stars gaze down, keepers of time,
In this sacred place, hearts quietly rhyme.

With each tide's return, hopes are renewed,
In whispers of the shore, love is imbued.
Forever I linger, in a soft embrace,
Where the ocean meets the endless space.

Ebb and Flow of Love

Like the tide that rolls and sways,
Our love dances in the sun's warm rays.
Sometimes crashing, sometimes calm,
In storms and stillness, we find our balm.

Moments of laughter, whispers so sweet,
Together we navigate each heartbeat.
When shadows fall, and doubts arise,
We learn to trust, to rise and defy.

In the ebb and flow, we find our way,
Building a bond that won't fade away.
Hand in hand, we chase the light,
Together, we soar, taking flight.

Through seasons of change, we stand as one,
In the dance of love, our journey begun.
No matter the storms, no matter the night,
In each other's arms, we always find light.

Driftwood Dreams

On the beach, driftwood waits,
Carved by waves, shaped by fates.
Stories linger in each rough line,
Of distant shores and heartbeat's sign.

Above the tide, the gulls take flight,
Chasing the colors of fading light.
Among the tangled roots and sand,
Lies the promise of a magic land.

In quiet moments, visions clear,
Dreams awaken, drawing near.
With every piece, a world restored,
Connections forged with nature's lore.

Beneath the stars, we gather and see,
Driftwood dreams, wild and free.
Each wave whispering to the shore,
Of journeys taken and so much more.

Secrets Beneath the Surface

Beneath the waves, a world hides deep,
Secrets ocean whispers as it sweeps.
Coral castles in a sapphire sea,
Echo stories of what used to be.

Fish dart swiftly through hidden lanes,
In shimmering light, freedom reigns.
With every ripple, a tale unfolds,
Of treasures buried and dreams retold.

Bubbles rise like hopes embraced,
In depths of blue, time is faced.
Together we dive, hearts intertwined,
In secrets shared, our souls aligned.

Emerging from depths, we breathe anew,
With each wave's return, love feels true.
In the dance of the tides and the moon's soft glow,
We find the truths we yearn to know.

Shelters from the Storm

In the heart of chaos bright,
Moments paused in waning light.
Walls embrace the weary soul,
Every shadow feels the whole.

Raindrops tap against the glass,
Whispers of a world that's passed.
Safe we hold, beneath the roof,
Finding stillness, timeless proof.

Though the winds may howl and scream,
Here we find a softer dream.
Wrapped in love, we stand as one,
Sheltered till the storm is done.

Navigating the Echoes

In the silence, echoes stray,
Whispers lost, they fade away.
Tracing footsteps, paths unwind,
Every sound, a thread to find.

Voices rise and overlap,
Stories told in a gentle clap.
Waves of memories gently surge,
In the ebb, our thoughts emerge.

Navigating through the haze,
Mapping out forgotten days.
With each echo, strength we gain,
Resilience found in joy and pain.

The Calm After the Storm

Once the tempest's rage is quelled,
In its wake, our hearts have swelled.
Gentle breezes start to play,
Softened light at break of day.

Colors bloom in morning's grace,
Nature smiles in a warm embrace.
Birds return with songs so sweet,
Life's moment, a soft heartbeat.

Behind us, shadows gently fade,
Lessons learned, the path we made.
In this calm, we breathe anew,
Holding tight to hope so true.

Rippling Emotions

In the stillness of the night,
Feelings dance in soft moonlight.
Waves of joy and waves of fear,
Echoing what's whispered clear.

Hearts like rivers softly flow,
With each pulse, we come to know.
Layers deep, the feelings rise,
Reflections caught in soulful eyes.

Fleeting moments, time will bend,
Unraveling what heart can mend.
In the ripples, stories gleaned,
Life, a tapestry weaved and dreamed.

Beneath Tempestuous Skies

Beneath tempestuous skies, we stand,
Clutching dreams in trembling hands.
The winds howl loud, the waves rise high,
As lightning dances in the blackened sky.

Whispers of the storm call out our names,
A symphony of fear, yet love remains.
We face the fury, hearts entwined,
In the tempest's arms, true strength we find.

Each thunderclap strikes like a drum,
Echoes of courage, for we won't succumb.
Together we weather, together we fight,
Beneath the chaos, we ignite our light.

When the clouds disperse and calm prevails,
We'll dance on shores where hope never fails.
Beneath tempestuous skies, we shall soar,
With dreams unfurled, forevermore.

A Heart Adrift

A heart adrift on the sea of doubt,
Waves of uncertainty swirling about.
In the silence, a voice calls clear,
Yet, in shadows, I still feel fear.

Drifting further from the shores I know,
Chasing whispers in the ebb and flow.
The stars above, shining so bright,
Guide me through the endless night.

With each current, I search for a sign,
A glimpse of love, a spark divine.
Behind the fog, a beacon shines,
A promise of solace in tangled vines.

But as the tide pulls me away,
I cling to hope, come what may.
A heart adrift, yet bold and free,
In the flow of life, I choose to be.

Lost in the Swell

Lost in the swell of the ocean's embrace,
Tossed in the currents, no familiar place.
The horizon blurs, a canvas of gray,
Each wave a whisper, leading astray.

Voices of the deep echo my name,
In depths unknown, nothing feels the same.
Glimmers of light flicker and fade,
As time drifts slowly, memories invade.

Yet in the chaos, a calm does dwell,
Where shadows linger, I weave my spell.
With every heartbeat, I search for ground,
In the labyrinth of waters, solace is found.

Though lost in the swell, I carry on,
Navigating the tide till the break of dawn.
For even in darkness, I find my way,
Embracing the journey, come what may.

Shoreline Reflections

At the shoreline, I gaze at the dawn,
Where whispers of waves weave truths long gone.
Footprints linger in the soft, wet sand,
Memories etched by a gentle hand.

Reflections shimmer in the morning light,
Each ripple a echo of day and night.
The horizon stretches, vast and wide,
With tales of journeys where dreams reside.

In the tide's embrace, I stand in awe,
Boundless love hidden in nature's jaw.
As seagulls soar and the breeze begins,
I feel the pulse of life's endless spins.

Shoreline reflections tell stories untold,
Of love and loss, both tender and bold.
In each wave's crash, a promise rings clear,
Life's endless beauty, eternally near.

A Sailor's Solace

Upon the waves, my heart takes flight,
The salty breeze, a sweet delight.
Stars above in endless night,
Guide me home, the world feels right.

With every tide, a story told,
Of dreams like ships, they brave the cold.
In solitude, the heart grows bold,
For in the sea, my soul unfolds.

A distant shore, a place of rest,
Where all my troubles lay to rest.
In gentle peace, I am blessed,
The ocean's call, forever pressed.

So here I sail, my fears at bay,
With every dawn, a brand new day.
The sea, my friend, will guide my way,
In sailor's solace, I shall stay.

The Depths of Connection

In whispered dreams, we intertwine,
Like roots of trees, our hearts align.
Through laughter shared and tears combined,
In every glance, our souls defined.

The currents of time, they ebb and flow,
Yet here we stand, our love will grow.
In every storm, in every glow,
Together strong, we boldly go.

A bond that deepens, vast and wide,
Like ocean depths, we cannot hide.
In every heartbeat, side by side,
In trust and love, we gently glide.

Through tides of change, we'll find our way,
In every night, and every day.
A dance of hearts, in sweet ballet,
In depths of love, we choose to stay.

Sheltered by the Moon

Beneath the glow of silver light,
My worries fade into the night.
The gentle waves, a soft embrace,
In moonlit dreams, I find my place.

The stars above, like whispered songs,
Remind me where my heart belongs.
In quiet moments, time extends,
Sheltered by the moon, where love transcends.

The nightingale sings sweet and low,
A serenade that makes hearts glow.
In twilight's hush, the world feels kind,
With every breath, our fates entwined.

So let us linger, hand in hand,
In silver shadows, we shall stand.
In moonlit dreams, we make our plans,
In this serene, enchanted land.

Rough Waters, Smooth Sailing

When storms arise and skies turn gray,
We anchor deep, we find our way.
With every wave that crashes hard,
We'll navigate, our hearts the card.

The tempest roars, yet we hold fast,
For love, we know, will surely last.
With every trial we face as one,
We find the strength, we've just begun.

Through rough waters, our spirits soar,
Each challenge faced just opens doors.
Smooth sailing waits beyond the fight,
Together bound by sheer delight.

So let it come, let tempests rage,
With every chapter, we turn the page.
The journey's ours, forever bold,
In rough waters, our tale is told.

Smooth Sailing

With gentle winds and sails that billow,
The horizon glows, a steady glow.
A path ahead, so bright and clear,
In smooth sailing, our hearts draw near.

The ocean's calm, a soothing balm,
With whispers soft, it brings a calm.
Together on this scenic ride,
With trust and love, we turn the tide.

The sun will set, but not for long,
With every note, we sing our song.
In tranquil seas, our spirits play,
In smooth sailing, we find our way.

So here's to dreams, and journeys grand,
With open hearts, we'll take a stand.
Embracing life, come what may,
In smooth sailing, we'll glide away.

Waves of Emotion

Roaring tides crash with grace,
Whispers of the heart's embrace.
Each swell tells a story bright,
Carving dreams in silver light.

The pull of love, a ceaseless flow,
Rising high, then sinking low.
In every wave, a chance we take,
A dance of joy, a heart that breaks.

The salty air, a bittersweet kiss,
Moments lost and found in bliss.
With each retreat, a longing grows,
A tide of feelings that ebbs and flows.

We surf the storms, we brave the fight,
Chasing the dawn, embracing night.
In the ocean vast, our truths collide,
Waves of emotion, our hearts confide.

The Currents Within

Silent whispers, deep and wide,
Hidden currents we cannot hide.
The heart's compass guides the way,
Through murky depths, night and day.

A river flows with ancient lore,
Secrets held on the ocean floor.
Each splash a tale of time gone by,
Echoes of laughter, a distant sigh.

Within these depths, storms may rise,
Yet calmness lingers in disguise.
In every ebb, a chance to heal,
Navigating what hearts conceal.

The currents pull, they drift, they sway,
Carving paths where shadows play.
In every ripple, love and fear,
The currents within draw us near.

Ocean of Longing

A vast expanse beneath the moon,
Waves of dreams, a silent tune.
Every crest, a whisper's plea,
In this ocean, longing frees.

Tidal whispers of hope and dread,
Drifting thoughts, the words unsaid.
In the solitude, we search and yearn,
An endless journey, with every turn.

Deep in the azure, treasures hide,
Fragments of love we can't abide.
As stars reflect on waters deep,
Promises made, and secrets keep.

This ocean calls with a gentle pull,
Hearts afloat, longing is full.
In the depths where wishes gleam,
We'll find solace in the dream.

Underneath the Surface

Beneath the calm, the wild resides,
Where sorrow swims and joy abides.
Hidden depths, a tale untold,
In quiet waves, our secrets fold.

Ebbing tides with restless hearts,
Navigating through the art of parts.
In silence deep, where shadows play,
The truth emerges, come what may.

We dive to seek what lies below,
Memories lost in the undertow.
With every breath, we break the cage,
Unravel spirits trapped in rage.

Underneath the surface, we explore,
The vast unknown, forevermore.
In waters dark, we learn to see,
The depth of life, the soul set free.